Mission to Mars

The Search For Life On Mars

John Hamilton

p

ABDO
Daughters & Publishing

Visit us at
www.abdopub.com

Published by Abdo Publishing Company, 4940 Viking Drive, Edina, MN 55435.
Copyright ©1998 by Abdo Consulting Group, Inc. International copyrights reserved in all countries. No part of this book may be reproduced in any form without written permission from the publisher.

Printed in the United States.

Interior Graphic Design: John Hamilton
Cover Design: MacLean & Tuminelly
Contributing Editors: Alan Gergen, Morgan Hughes

Cover photo: NASA/JPL
Interior photos: NASA/JPL

Sources: Caidin, Martin & Barbree, Jay. *Destination Mars*. New York: Penguin Studio, 1997; Jet Propulsion Laboratory, Public Information Office, California Institute of Technology, Pasadena, CA; NASA website. http://nssdc.gsfc.nasa.gov/planetary/planets/marspage.html; Sagen, Carl. *Cosmos*. New York: Random House, 1980.

Library of Congress Cataloging–in–Publication Data

Hamilton, John, 1959-
   The search for life on Mars / John Hamilton
      p. cm. — (Mission to Mars)
   Includes index.
   Summary: Describes the discovery of a meteorite suggesting to scientists that primitive life may have existed on the planet Mars over three billion years ago.
   ISBN 1-56239-830-X
   1. Mars (Planet)—Geology—Juvenile literature.   2. Life on other planets—Juvenile literature. [1. Mars (Planet) 2. Life on other planets.] I. Title.
II. Series: Hamilton, John, 1959-, Mission to Mars.
QB641.H314 1998
576.8'39'09923—dc21   97-34680
                                       CIP
                                       AC

CONTENTS

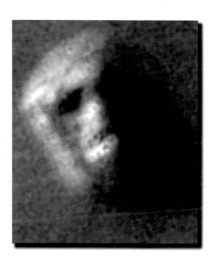

CHAPTER 1
· · · · · · · · · · · · · · ·
LIFE ON MARS?

When ancient civilizations first started paying attention to the night sky, there was one planet in particular that held their fascination. It both mesmerized and terrified them. The planet was Mars, a blood-red speck in the sky that sometimes wandered among the constellations as if it had a mind of its own. Today we know that this erratic movement is an illusion, an effect called "retrograde motion," which we see as Earth and Mars travel through space on their separate orbits around the sun. But ancient people didn't know this—to them, Mars became a god. To the Greeks and Romans, the Red Planet was the God of War, a powerful force to be feared and respected.

Much later in history, when technology allowed us to gaze deeper into the heavens with telescopes, Mars once again held our rapt attention. In 1877, when "canals" were discovered on the surface of Mars by Italian astronomer Giovanni Schiaparelli, people were positive that some sort of advanced civilization thrived on the Red Planet. Countless stories arose in popular literature of Martians coming to Earth. Some of the aliens were friendly, but most were not, especially the heat-ray-wielding invaders of H.G. Wells' "War of the Worlds."

Toward the end of this century, when space probes shattered the myth of Martian canals and advanced

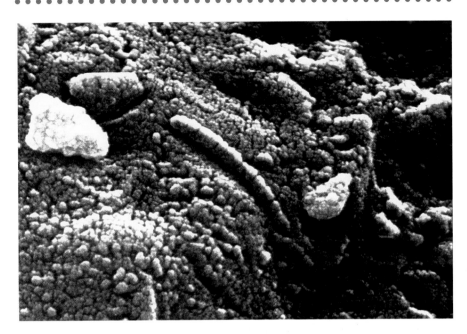

This electron microscope scan shows a possible bacteria-like microfossil. It was found inside a meteorite scientists say came from Mars. Does this prove life once existed on Mars?

civilizations (or, for that matter, any life at all on that sterile, hostile world), many people felt strangely disappointed. But not for long. New theories cropped up to replace the old. Are those "pyramids" and an ancient "sphinx" showing up on Viking space probe photographs? And could it be that fossils embedded in a Martian meteorite prove the existence of life on that remote, forbidding planet?

And so the debate continues; is there life on Mars? Has there ever been? It may seem strange, in this era of high technology, when we're on the very brink of a new millenium, that humankind still obsesses with the possibility of life on our sister planet. But if there's one truth out there, it's this—people want to believe.

CHAPTER 2
·················
THE MARTIAN CANALS

Mars is the fourth planet from the sun, the second closest to Earth (Venus is the closest). It's only about half the size of Earth, but because there are no oceans of liquid water, Mars has about the same land surface area as Earth. Mars' reddish appearance is due to a coating of iron oxide minerals (which cause rust on Earth). Each planet has ice-covered poles, and days that last about 24 hours. But Mars has a very thin atmosphere (95 percent carbon dioxide), and bone-chilling temperatures that can plunge to –255 Fahrenheit (–125 C).

Astronomers of the late nineteenth and early twentieth centuries didn't know most of these details. But even with

their crude telescopes, they could see Mars' poles, and could tell that the Red Planet had seasons, like we do on Earth. If any other place in our solar system harbored life, it seemed like Mars was the best bet.

Left: Astronomer Percival Lowell in his Flagstaff, Arizona, observatory. *Facing page:* Mars, the Red Planet.

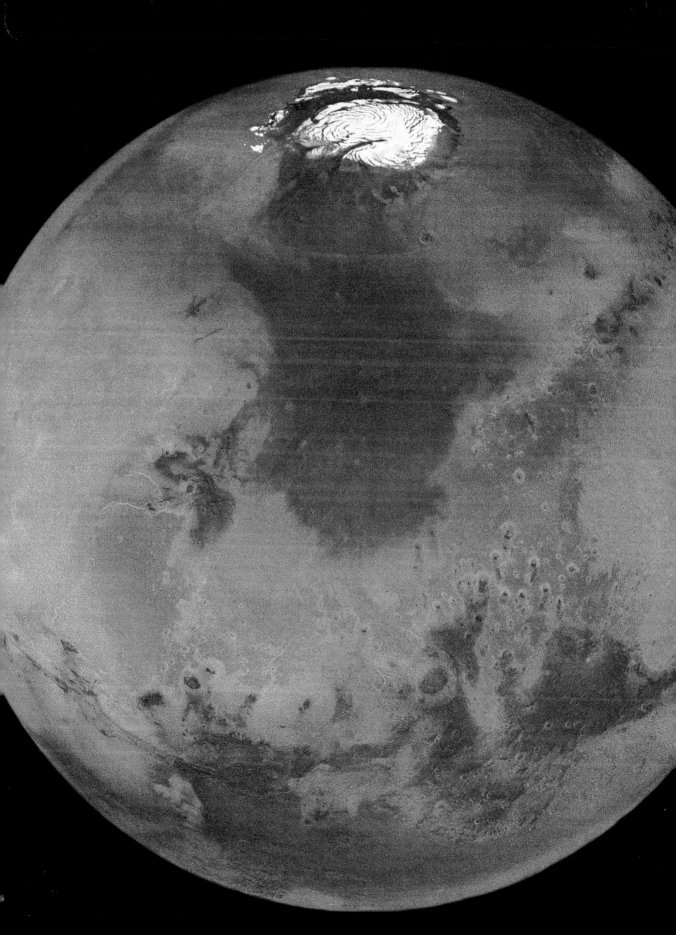

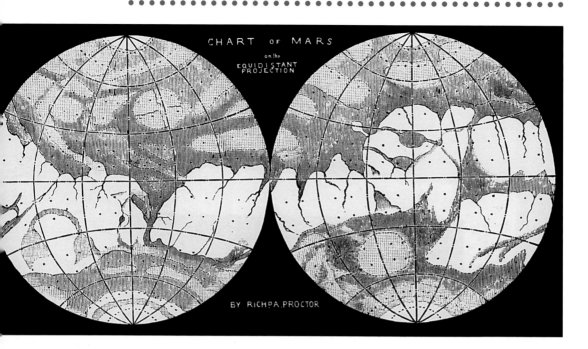

CHART OF MARS
on the
EQUIDISTANT PROJECTION

BY RICHARD A. PROCTOR

A chart of Mars made by combining the drawings of Schiaparelli and other astronomers.

In 1877, Italian astronomer Giovanni Schiaparelli trained his 8-inch (20 cm) telescope on Mars. With his sharp eyesight, he observed what looked like a network of lines running across the planet's surface. When he announced his discovery, he called these grooves "canali," which in Italian means "channels," or "grooves." The rest of the world misunderstood, however, and thought that Schiaparelli had discovered "canals" on Mars. Soon people were convinced that the canals were proof of an advanced civilization on the Red Planet.

Another astronomer, American Percival Lowell, dedicated many years of his life to proving the existence of life on Mars. From his large mountain observatory near Flagstaff, Arizona, Lowell was convinced that he, too, could see canals running across the surface of Mars. Though he wasn't able to offer any real proof of his findings, he was popular with the public. People were convinced that there *must* be alien life on Mars. Popular fiction reinforced this idea, including H.G. Wells' 1897 masterpiece, *War of the Worlds*.

Finally, in July 1965, the U.S. space probe *Mariner 4* zoomed past the Red Planet, sending back to Earth 22 images of the surface of Mars. People were shocked at what they saw: instead of oceans and forests, there was desert. Instead of cities, only craters. Not a single canal could be seen. Schiaparelli's "canali" had almost certainly been optical illusions.

Mars was dead.

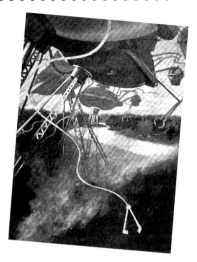

A Warwick Goble illustration from the 1897 *Pearson's Magazine* original publication of H.G. Wells' *War of the Worlds*.

The crater-filled photos taken by the early Mariner 4 missions reinforced the idea that Mars had a dead, lunar-like surface.

CHAPTER 3

THE VIKING MISSIONS

When *Mariner 9* mapped Mars in 1971 and 1972, NASA scientists were in for a big surprise. Instead of the dead, crater-filled landscapes that the previous Mariner missions had recorded, a different kind of Mars emerged. Enormous volcanoes rose up off the northern plains, and a giant rift valley, Vallis Marineris, stretched nearly 3,000 miles (4,827 km) long.

Most exciting of all, however, was evidence of water in Mars' distant past. Water is a necessary ingredient for life as we know it. Ancient riverbeds clearly cut across the planet's surface. Scientists wondered, if water once flowed freely across Mars, did life evolve, just as it did on Earth? The only way to tell was to send a probe to the surface of the Red Planet, and this is exactly what NASA did.

In July 1976, nearly a year after their launch from Earth, twin space probes, *Viking 1* and *Viking 2*, landed on Mars. They were technological marvels for their time. Each lander was packed with high-tech gear, cameras, and science labs designed to detect even the slightest hint of life on Mars. The landers scooped up samples of Martian soil and chemically analyzed them. At first, a promising reaction was detected, but NASA decided that

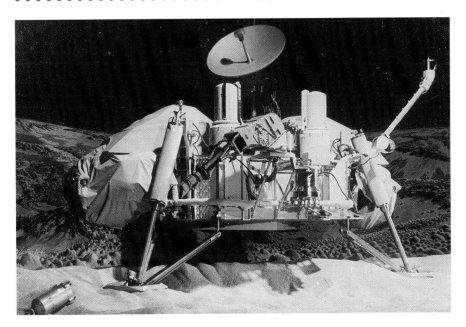

A mockup of a Viking lander.

it was just an exotic chemical reaction in the soil itself, not evidence of Martian microbes.

Based on data sent back from the landers, few scientists were surprised that the soil sample experiments failed to detect life. Mars was a harsh, severely cold place. Water cannot exist on the surface of the planet in liquid form. Deadly ultraviolet radiation from the sun bombards the planet's surface. It would have been a miracle if life had been detected in such a hostile place. It was very discouraging.

And yet. . .

Many scientists refuse to rule out the possibility of life on Mars. After all, the Viking probes only sampled soil from two spots on the planet's surface. Perhaps life evolved long ago in Mars' history, but has now taken refuge in underground reservoirs of water that we haven't yet detected. Mars once held the ingredients for life. There are many possibilities still to be explored. For many planetary scientists, Mars is still an open book.

CHAPTER 4

THE FACE OF CYDONIA

During the summer of 1976, the *Viking 1* orbiter was busy taking medium-resolution photographs of the surface of Mars. NASA scientists were searching for an alternate landing site for the *Viking 2* lander. During one of its orbits, *Viking 1* passed over the flat plains of Cydonia, which sits in the Northern Hemisphere of Mars. The orbiter's cameras dutifully recorded surface details as the planet swooped by underneath.

Soon scientists at NASA's Jet Propulsion Laboratory (JPL), which oversaw the Viking program, poured over the photographs beamed back to Earth from the orbiter. When they looked at frame number 35A72, they were met with a big surprise. Staring back at them was a helmeted humanoid face, gazing up into space.

Facing page: The "Face" of Cydonia: a trick of light playing on an eroded mountain, or evidence of an ancient civilization on Mars?

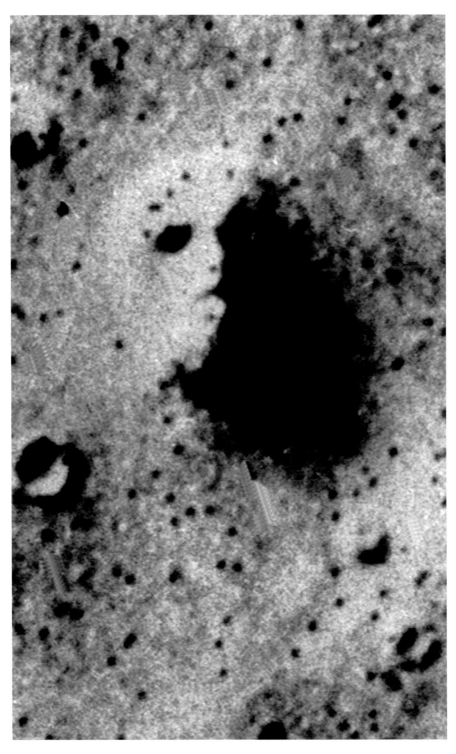

The "Face" on Mars is an eroded rock formation that measures about 1.55 miles (2.5 km) long, 1.24 miles (2.0 km) wide, and .25 miles (.4 km) tall. The Cydonia region is located on the boundary between ancient highlands and low-lying plains. Eroded rock formations are all that is left of the highlands that once covered the area, much like the mesas and buttes of the desert Southwest United States. It is a geologically interesting place to explore, even without the mysterious Face.

When it was first discovered, scientists at JPL dismissed it as simply a trick of lighting angles, with shadows in the rocks giving the illusion of a nose and mouth. Image 35A72 is also speckled in appearance. These small black dots are called "bit errors," and represent missing data that was lost as the signal was transmitted from Mars to Earth. Coincidentally, part of one of the eyes and a nostril on the Face are made of bit errors, heightening the illusion of a humanoid appearance. After deciding the Face was a purely natural phenomenon, frame 35A72 was filed and seemingly forgotten.

Several years later, two engineers at NASA's Goddard Spaceflight Center rediscovered the image. They also found another image (frame 70A13) that showed the Face under different lighting conditions. During the early 1980s, computer imaging helped bring out more details, including features in the shadowed right side of the Face. Fine lines in the mouth area resemble teeth.

The Face is not an isolated feature—several other curious structures are seen in the same area. These include a series of "pyramids," and what appear to be the remains of an ancient city, or fortress. (Of course, these

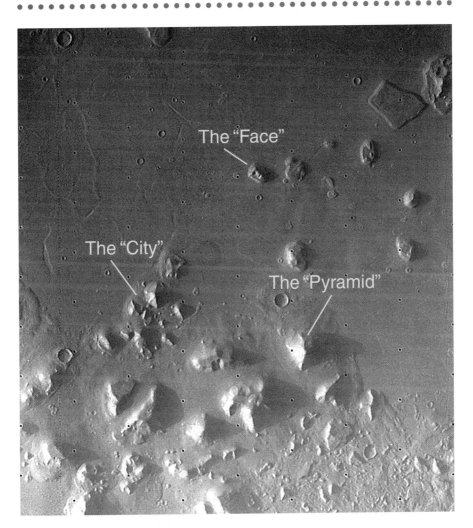

The "Face"

The "City"

The "Pyramid"

are all in the eye of the beholder. Some people just see a jumble of rocks.)

The Face of Cydonia, plus the other artifacts, suddenly became a hot topic in popular literature. Many people, including some trained scientists, concluded that the features of Cydonia proved the existence of an advanced civilization on Mars. Several books were written presenting wild theories about the origins of the Face. Some believe a long-dead race of Martians left the Face behind as a monument to their civilization (much like the

A Viking orbiter image showing the Face and two other "artifacts," an ancient city and a pyramid. (Or perhaps just a jumble of huge rocks.)

Left: A narrow section of Mars photographed by the *Mars Global Surveyor* spacecraft during April 1998. The Face of Cydonia is at the top of the image.
Facing page: The *Mars Global Surveyor* spacecraft.

pyramids and sphinx of the ancient Egyptians). Others firmly believe that aliens from some other part of our galaxy left the face on Mars as a message to Earth. One theory even says that there is a mathematical relationship in the distance between the artifacts, and that if we can descramble the numbers in just the right way, we'll unlock the alien secrets of a powerful new energy source!

Most trained scientists say this is all just plain silly. They insist that the Face looks like a human because of a coincidence in lighting and natural erosion. We know that on Mars there is wind and seismic activity (Mars quakes), and that in the planet's ancient past running water contributed to erosion. These scientists think it much more likely that this combination of events carved the Face of Cydonia.

NASA's firm stance that the Face is a result of natural forces has caused an

unexpected result: many people think that the United States government is trying to cover up the truth. These conspiracy theorists believe that NASA really has discovered proof of aliens on Mars, and that the truth is too horrible and frightening to tell the rest of the world. As further "proof," the conspiracy buffs point to the *Mars Observer* mission in August of 1993, which failed hours before it was to enter orbit around the Red Planet. *Observer* was supposed to begin high-resolution imaging of the planet's surface, including the Cydonia region. Some think that the government destroyed the probe on purpose, rather than let the rest of the world know the terrible "truth" it was about to uncover. Some people even think that Martians blew up *Observer!*

NASA, of course, refuses to back down. The space agency says these conspiracy theories are nonsense. (The official explanation of *Observer's* failure was that a fuel line probably burst shortly before entering Mars orbit.)

And yet, if the Face of Cydonia *is* artificial, if it *is* some sort of ancient monument, it would be one of the greatest discoveries in human history. Even though most scientists scoff at the suggestion that the Face is a relic of some ancient civilization, they do admit that there isn't enough proof to rule the theory out completely. They say they need to examine the data from higher resolution images of the area. (Some scientists, though, say that we will never be able to tell *for sure* unless we land astronauts on the surface of Mars and explore up close.)

The next spacecraft scheduled to explore the Red Planet is the *Mars Global Surveyor* probe. If all goes well, *Surveryor* will begin high-resolution imaging of the planet's surface sometime in the spring of 1999. Because of the enormous interest in the Cydonia features, NASA plans to take images from the region and make them public immediately. (Actually, there are public relations reasons for this as well. NASA is determined not to come across as a suppressor of the "truth," and hopes to satisfy the people who are making accusations against the space agency.) NASA also says there are good scientific reasons for photographing the Cydonia region, which is why the *Viking 1* probe explored the area in the first place in 1976.

In April 1998, *Mars Global Surveyor* took detailed images of the Cydonia region. (The probe must go through a long "aerobraking" procedure, which slows it down enough to put it in its final orbit around Mars. Scientists took advantage of the aerobraking by taking photos during the probe's closest approach to the planet.)

This time, with the sun at a different angle, and with a higher resolution camera, the Face of Cydonia didn't look much like a face anymore. Instead, it looked exactly like what the scientists had been saying all along—an eroded mesa with a straight edge.

Already controversy is brewing. Many insist that the Face is artificial, that it's eroded just like many ancient structures here on Earth, like ancient cities in the Middle East or Central America. They point to the straight edges as their proof. Others are sure that NASA somehow altered the picture. They say that the space agency knows about the aliens that built the Face, but doesn't want to panic the public. We may never know *for sure* whether the structure is artificial until we send a team of astronauts to investigate the site.

Meanwhile, the Face of Cydonia stares blankly toward the heavens, as it has for untold centuries, watching and waiting.

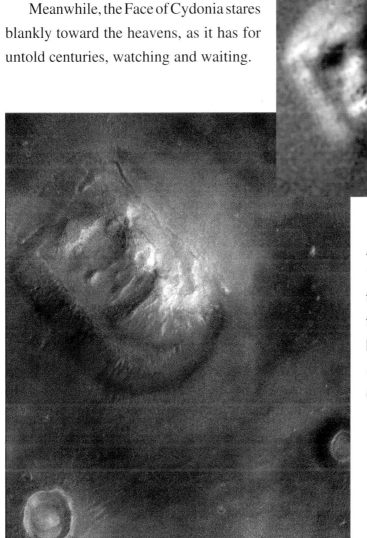

A comparison of the 1976 Viking image of the Face (above) and the 1998 image taken by the *Mars Global Surveyor* spacecraft (left).

CHAPTER 5

· · · · · · · · · · · · · ·

MARTIAN METEORITES

The gloved hand of a NASA technician holds meteorite ALH84001, which scientists have determined came from Mars.

O n August 6, 1996, NASA announced, after a two-year investigation, a startling discovery: "A NASA research team of scientists at the Johnson Space Center (JSC) and at Stanford University has found evidence that strongly suggests primitive life may have existed on Mars more than 3.6 billion years ago."

The announcement referred to a 4.2-pound (1.9-kg), potato-sized meteorite found in Antarctica, which scientists determined came from Mars. They named this meteorite ALH84001. The research team included planetary scientist Dr. David McKay. "There is not any one finding that leads us to believe that this is evidence of past life on Mars," McKay said. "Rather, it is a combination of many things that we have found."

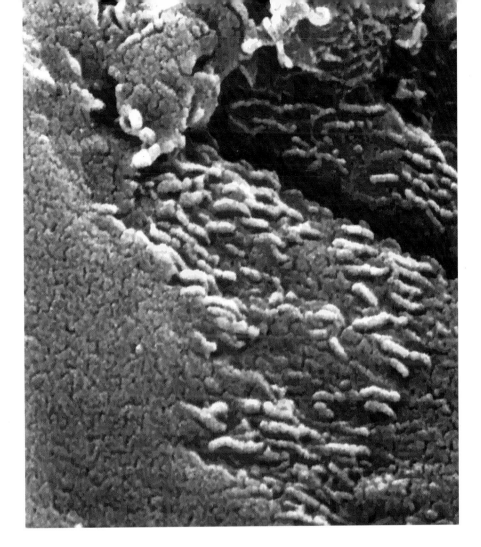

The "evidence" of primitive life that the NASA team discovered on ALH84001 comes in several forms. They found organic (carbon-based) molecules in the meteorite. (Carbon molecules are the basic building blocks of all life as we know it.) They also found mineral features that hinted at biological activity. Most exciting of all, by using electron microscopes and other advanced imaging technology (laser mass spectrometry), the team discovered what appears to be the fossilized remains of ancient bacteria. These tube-like microfossils are very small. If you placed 100 of the largest microfossils end to end, they would still be smaller than the width of a human hair.

An electron microscope view of a section of ALH84001. The tube-like structures might be microfossils, or they could merely be crystals.

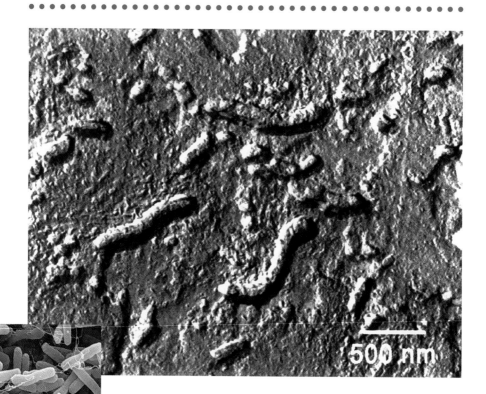

Possible Martian microfossils from meteorite ALH84001 (top), shown with E. coli bacteria from Earth (bottom).

Dr. Everett Gibson, another planetary scientist on the NASA team, said, "For two years, we have applied state-of-the-art technology to perform these analyses, and we believe we have found quite reasonable evidence of past life on Mars. We don't claim that we have conclusively proven it. We are putting this evidence out to the scientific community for other investigators to verify, enhance, attack—disprove if they can—as part of the scientific process. Then, within a year or two, we hope to resolve the question one way or the other."

The debate has begun already. Dozens of independent studies have both attacked and supported the NASA team's conclusions. One research study suggested in January, 1998, that most of the organic carbon molecules in the meteorite probably didn't come from Mars. This means that most of the carbon material is contamination from Earth. However, a small part of the carbon almost certainly came from Mars, so the microfossils, if that's what they are, still *could* be from the Red Planet.

One of the first questions people ask when they hear the news about the fossils in the Mars meteorite, is how do they know the meteorite is from Mars? And how did it get to Earth, anyway?

ALH84001 was found in 1984 in Antarctica, which is the best place in the world to search for meteorites. NASA co-sponsors a group called ANSMET (the Antarctic Search for Meteorites). So far over 7,500 meteorite samples have been collected. That's a lot, considering only 2,500 meteorites have ever been discovered outside Antarctica.

Antarctica is a great place for meteorite hunting, not because more fall there than anywhere else, but because it's so much easier to find them there. If a meteorite falls in the ocean, it's lost. If it falls on land, it can be hard to see among all the other rocks or vegetation. But in Antarctica meteorites are a lot easier to see. When a meteorite falls in Antarctica, it is quickly covered by snow and ice, and is preserved by the harsh cold.

ANSMET members in Antarctica looking for meteorites in "blue ice."

After many, many years (sometimes millions) the meteorite may become part of an Antarctic glacier, encased in a layer of "blue ice." (All the air bubbles are squeezed out of the ice by the immense pressure of the glacier, which turns it blue.) Members of ANSMET slowly travel over glaciers, looking for rocks that might be meteorites encased in blue ice. The team members usually use snowmobiles on the hard, slippery surface. Snowmobiles also help protect them from falling into hidden, narrow crevasses hundreds of feet deep.

When a meteorite is found, the ANSMET team uses high-tech gear to get it out of the rock-hard ice. They are very careful not to contaminate the meteorite, using only stainless steel instruments. Once the meteorite is freed, it is sealed in a bag, packed in dry ice, and sent to the Antarctic Meteorite Laboratory at the Johnson Space Center, in Houston, Texas.

In 1984, U.S. geologist and ANSMET team member Roberta Score found a meteorite in the far western icefield of the Allan Hills Region of Antarctica. The meteorite was named ALH84001 (ALH stands for Allan Hills, and the 84 stands for the year of its discovery). Score thought the meteorite might be special because of its pale greenish color. Once back at the Meteorite Lab in Houston, however, ALH84001 was labeled a "common" meteorite and put into storage.

In 1993, scientists discovered that ALH84001 was no common meteorite— it was from Mars! They knew it was from the Red Planet because of tiny amounts of gases trapped inside the rock. Scientists

An ANSMET team member patrols a glacier on a snowmobile, looking for meteorites.

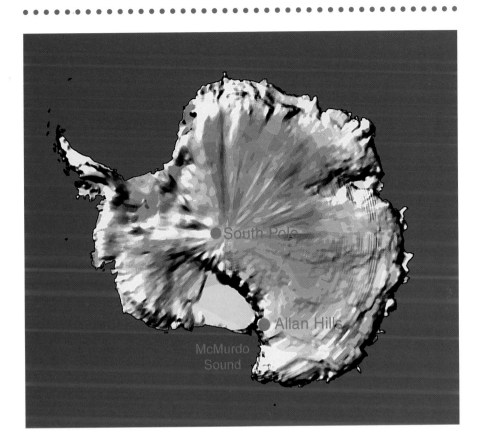

analyzed the gases and found an exact match with the atmosphere on Mars. (We know what the atmosphere on Mars is like because it was measured in 1976 by the *Viking 1* and *Viking 2* landers. Mars has unusual amounts of nitrogen, argon, krypton, and xenon in its air.) ALH84001 became one of only 12 Martian meteorites discovered so far.

Further study showed that ALH84001 is 4.5 billion years old, which makes it older than any rock ever found on Earth. It is almost as old as Mars itself. (Scientists estimate that Mars is 4.55 billion years old.) But how did it get to Earth? There is only one logical explanation that planetary scientists can give. Long ago, a huge asteroid or

A map of Antarctica showing the Allan Hills region, where the Mars meteorite ALH84001 was discovered.

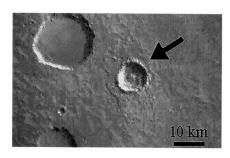

The arrow in this photo points to what scientists think is one likely spot where an asteroid slammed into Mars, blasting ALH84001 into space.

10 km

comet hit the surface of Mars with tremendous force. Rocks and debris from the impact crater were hurled into outer space. (By analyzing other chemicals on ALH84001, scientists think this impact happened about 16 million years ago.)

Finally, after wandering through space for all those millions of years, ALH84001 encountered Earth's atmosphere and fell in Antarctica. Scientists used a technique called carbon 14 dating and discovered that the meteorite spent 13,000 years trapped in the Antarctic ice before being found by the ANSMET team.

How can there be fossils of life in a rock that's so old? Actually, fossil bacteria have been found on Earth that are estimated to be 3.5 billion years old, so life on Mars *could* have evolved very early in the planet's history.

Some people wonder how life could have formed on such a barren, desolate place as Mars. After all, how could anything survive in the bone-chilling cold that exists there today? And how can life thrive on a planet with an atmosphere so thin and cold that liquid water cannot exist? But remember, early in its history Mars had a thicker atmosphere, and water flowed freely. We have proof of this from the images taken by the Mariner and Viking space probes. Ancient riverbeds are clearly visible. Also, huge volumes of water were once hidden beneath the surface of Mars; we know this because of "sploosh" craters, where slushy mud-like material flows outward from meteorite impact zones.

But even in its ancient history, the climate of Mars was probably quite harsh. Once again, however, we can find examples of life thriving in the most extreme of conditions, right here on Earth. Life is abundant even in volcanic vents, like the hot springs and geysers found in Yellowstone National Park. And recently a team of scientists discovered bacterial life that lives miles underground in the basalt lava rocks of eastern Washington state. There are many other examples, and because of this it isn't too much of a stretch of the imagination to think that life could have sprung up on the surface of ancient Mars.

But even so, why should we care about the possible existence of bacteria that lived billions of years ago on another planet? Because the origin of life as we know it is one of the greatest questions that science has yet to answer. How does life begin? What kinds of complex chemical reactions are needed before life can take hold? How common is life in the universe? By studying ALH84001, perhaps we can answer some of these questions, instead of merely guessing.

Much work has yet to be done to prove that ALH84001 holds microfossils of ancient Martian life. There is still much controversy. Many trained scientists insist that the structures inside the meteorite are nothing more than mineral grains that have the same shape and size as microfossils. NASA scientists hope to cut open one of the microfossils and find remnants of DNA strands, which would prove without a doubt that they

A "sploosh" crater, which hints that Mars once held large amounts of underground water.

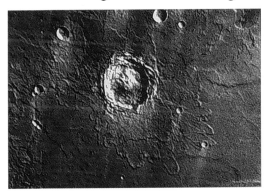

are indeed ancient lifeforms. But because the microfossils are so small it will be an extremely difficult process using today's technology.

Another way to prove the existence (or nonexistence) of life on Mars, either living or fossilized, is to somehow bring back rocks from the Red Planet directly. NASA hopes to send a spaceship to Mars within the next 5 to 10 years to do just that. It would collect samples, then blast off and return to Earth, where the rocks could be studied to find more information about possible life on Mars.

If scientists ever do prove that the meteorite from Mars contains evidence of ancient life, it will be very important news indeed. As President Bill Clinton said after NASA's first announcement in 1996, "Today rock 84001 speaks to us across all those billions of years and millions of miles. If this discovery is confirmed, it will surely be one of the most stunning insights into our universe that science has ever recorded."

An artist's rendering of a Mars return vehicle blasting off toward Earth with a cargo of Martian soil and rock samples.

INTERNET SITES

Starchild: A learning center for young astronomers
http://starchild.gsfc.nasa.gov/

This lively site, a service of the Laboratory for High Energy Astrophysics at NASA, is full of information on the solar system, astronauts, and space travel. It has a very good section on Mars covering the main features of the Red Planet, including photos.

Mars Missions
http://mpfwww.jpl.nasa.gov/

This NASA web page provides up-to-the-minute information and photographs on three current space probes: *Mars Pathfinder*, *Mars Global Surveyor*, and *Mars Surveyor 98*.

The Whole Mars Catalog
http://www.reston.com/astro/mars/catalog.html

This is a very extensive site of Mars facts and photos, with many links to other related web sites. Some of the many topics include Mars facts, breaking news from NASA, space probes, and the push to put humans on Mars.

These sites are subject to change. Go to your favorite search engine and type in "Mars" for more sites.

PASS IT ON

Space buffs: educate readers around the country by passing on information you've learned about Mars and space exploration. Share your little-known facts and interesting stories. We want to hear from you!

To get posted on the ABDO & Daughters website, E-mail us at "Science@abdopub.com"

Visit the ABDO & Daughters website at www.abdopub.com

GLOSSARY

probe

A probe is an unmanned space vehicle that is sent on missions that are too dangerous, or would take too long, for human astronauts to accomplish. Probes are equipped with many scientific instruments, like cameras and radiation detectors. Information from these instruments is radioed back to ground controllers on Earth.

rocket

A vehicle that moves because of the ejection of gases made by the burning of a self-contained propellant. The propellant is made up of fuel, like liquid hydrogen, and an oxidant like liquid oxygen, which helps the fuel to burn. Sometimes solid explosives are used, like nitroglycerin and nitrocellulose. Solid-fuel rockets are more reliable, but generate less thrust. Some spacecraft, like the United States' Space Shuttle, use a combination of solid and liquid fuel rocket boosters. Rockets were probably invented by the Chinese almost 1,000 years ago, when they stuffed gunpowder into bamboo pipes to make weapons.

solar panel

Many space probes use solar panels, which are large arrays of connected solar cells, to generate electricity. Solar cells are semiconductor devices that convert the energy of sunlight into electric energy. Electricity is needed to power the probe's science experiments, guidance systems, and radios. Some probes, especially those that travel far from the sun to explore the outer planets, rely on internal nuclear power plants to generate electricity. The *Cassini* probe to Saturn, launched in October of 1997 and due to arrive in 2004, uses a nuclear generator.

solar system

The sun, the nine planets, and other celestial bodies (like asteroids) that orbit the sun. The nine planets are (in order from the sun): Mercury, Venus, Earth, Mars, Jupiter, Saturn, Uranus, Neptune, and Pluto.

spectrometer

An instrument that determines what an unknown object is made of by analyzing how it reacts to the bombardment of an "energy spectrum," like heat or X-rays. Each of the known elements has its own special spectrum "signature," so by comparing these to the results of a spectrometer we can tell the chemical makeup of an unknown object.

star

A large, self-containing ball of gas that is "self luminous," or emits light. Stars come in many sizes, ranging from white dwarfs to red giants. The sun is a medium-sized yellow star. At night, stars are seen as twinkling points of light, which is one way to tell them apart from planets, which do not twinkle.

telescope

A device to detect and observe distant objects by their reflection or emission of various kinds of electromagnetic radiation (like light). Most astronomy research today is conducted with telescopes that detect electromagnetic radiation other than visible light, such as radio or x-ray telescopes.

INDEX